DESTINATION: JUPITER

SALLY SPRAY AND
MARK RUFFLE

WAYLAND

First published in Great Britain in 2023
by Wayland
© Hodder and Stoughton Limited, 2023

All rights reserved.

PB ISBN: 978 1 5263 2080 3

Editor: Paul Rockett
Design and illustration: Mark Ruffle
www.rufflebrothers.com

Manufactured, printed and assembled
in Dubai, UAE
First printing, April 2024 OP/04/24
28 27 26 25 24 1 2 3 4 5 6

Wayland
An imprint of Hachette Children's Group
Part of Hodder & Stoughton
Carmelite House
50 Victoria Embankment
London EC4Y 0DZ

A Hachette UK company
www.hachette.co.uk
www.hachettechildrens.co.uk

The website addresses (URLs) included in this book were valid at the time of going to press. However, it is possible that contents or addresses may have changed since the publication of this book. No responsibility for any such changes can be accepted by either the author or the Publisher.

Picture credits:
Page 30 GSFC/NASA; JPL/NASA;
page 31 JPL/NASA; NASA/JPL/DLR

SAFETY PRECAUTIONS
We recommend adult supervision at all times while doing the experiments in this book. Always be aware that ingredients may contain allergens, so check the packaging for allergens if there is a risk of an allergic reaction. Anyone with a known allergy must avoid these.
- Wear an apron and cover surfaces.
- Tie back long hair.
- Ask an adult for help with cutting.
- Check all ingredients for allergens.
- Clear up all spills right away.

Contents

- **4–27** Destination: Jupiter
- **28** Space Academy Activities
- **31** Further Information
- **32** Glossary and Index

Meet the team

Welcome to Space Station Academy, the amazing interstellar school that travels through space. Come on board and learn about our solar system.

Jumping Jupiter! We're nearly there! Why so glum, cadets?

Today, the Academy is nearing Jupiter and Dr. Bott is buzzing with excitement. The students however, are bored.

swum in the pool until our arms ached...

climbed the wall 20 times ...

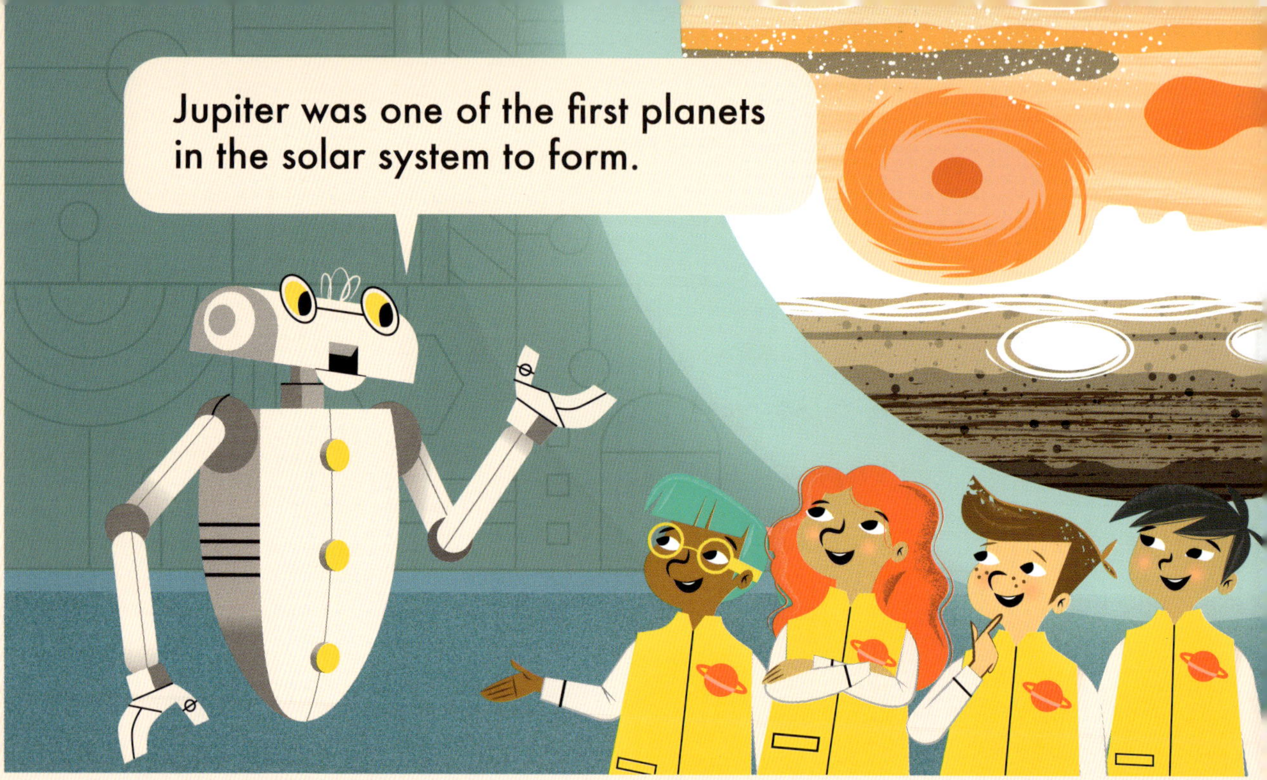
Jupiter was one of the first planets in the solar system to form.

It has a rocky core, but it became ginormous by pulling together lots of dust and gas.

Back then, Jupiter did not have a set orbit. It spiraled inward toward the Sun, gathering rocks and gas and growing as it traveled.

It moved as far forward as the young planet Mars and collected material that otherwise might have made the inner planets bigger.

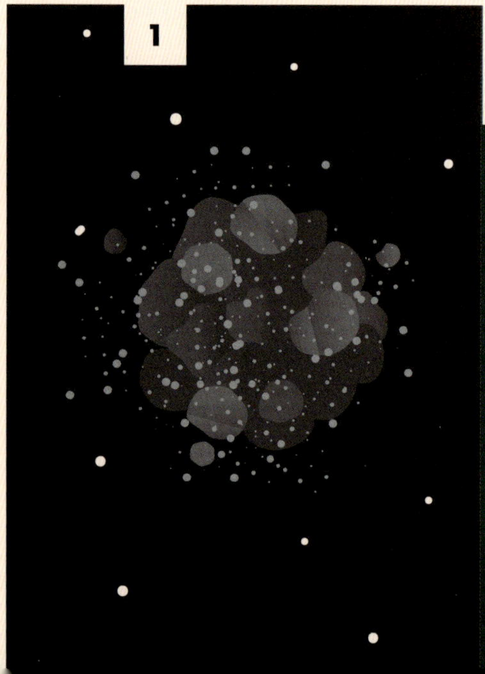
1

2
Sun
Mars
Jupiter

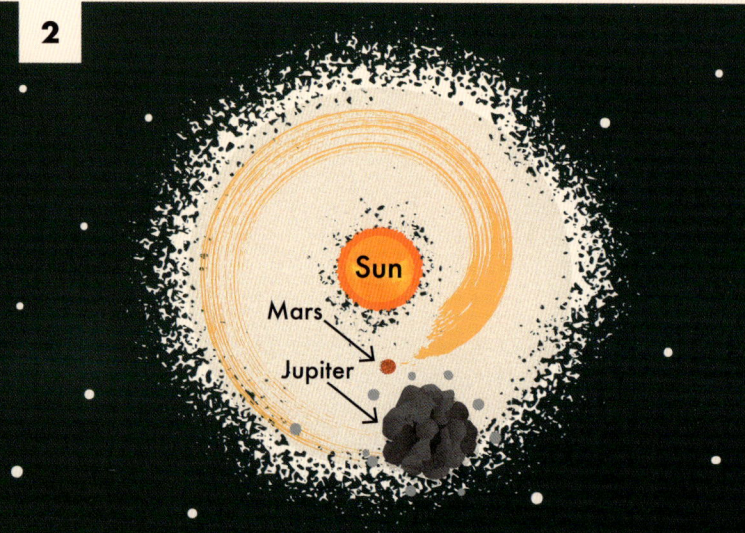

Jupiter then began to move outward and settled into position in the outer regions of the solar system.

As Jupiter moved through the asteroid belt, it knocked icy comets toward Earth, where they landed, melting into oceans.

Jupiter has gravity that is strong enough to capture passing comets and asteroids, sucking them into its churning atmosphere and crushing them to bits.

There isn't a solid surface beyond the clouds, just layers and layers of liquid gas and a core of liquid metal.

Does that mean we can't land on Jupiter? Boring! When does the adventure start?

It's made from hydrogen and helium, the same gases that make up the Sun. If Jupiter had grown bigger, about 75 percent bigger, it might have become a star.

The gases are moving constantly—cooling gas falls down and heated gas rises. When they meet they become giant storms. The weather on Jupiter is never calm!

This is so much fun!

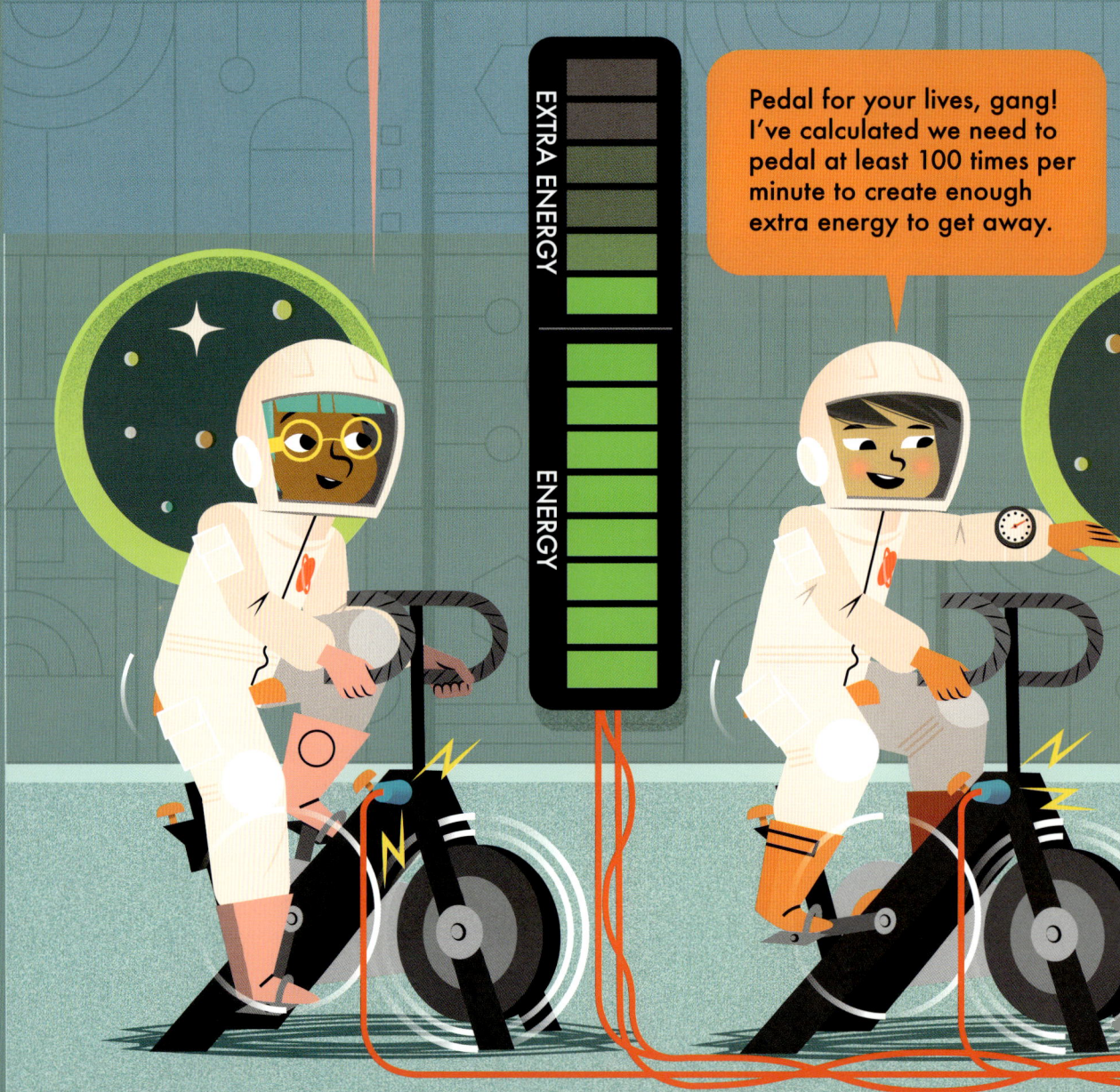

The space pod makes it safely away from Jupiter.

Look, my super cyclists—Jupiter has rings!

We're very lucky to see them. They're only visible when the Sun is behind Jupiter and the faint rings are illuminated in the light.

There are four in all, made from dust coming off meteors crashing into the atmosphere.

Some of Jupiter's small moons orbit within the rings. Adrastea and Metis are located in the main ring, while Amalthea and Thebe orbit in the Gossamer rings.

Space Academy Activities

The Space Academy gang have been so inspired by their mission to Jupiter, they wanted to find out more. Will you join them?

Dr. Bott's Space Experiment

Here's how to make your very own Red Spot Storm! Ask an adult for permission to do this activity.

Equipment
- Two large plastic bottles, of the same size
- Metal washer—bigger than the bottle opening
- Tape—thick wide tape will work best
- Water
- Red food coloring

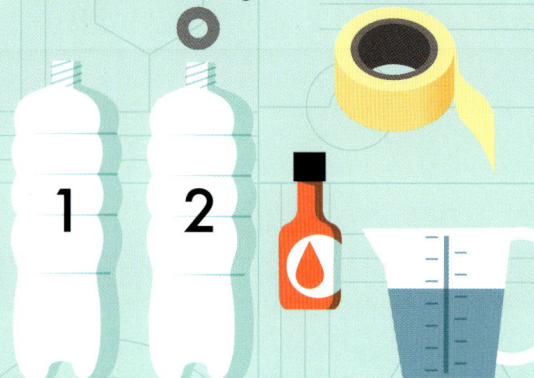

Method
Fill one bottle half full with water (bottle 1).

Add a couple of drops of food coloring or paint.

Dry the top.

Put the washer on the top of the bottle.

Place the other bottle (bottle 2) upside down on the top of bottle 1 and the washer.

Tape the two bottles together, **securely**.

Outcomes
Turn the bottles over and rotate slightly. The water from bottle 1 will move into bottle 2 creating a tornado effect as it goes.

Experiment variations
Try less water in your bottle. Try a mix of oil and water. What happens if you don't rotate the objects? Do you get the same effect?

Melody's Jupiter Fact

You can see Jupiter in the night sky from Earth. Find out where to look in the sky from your location and see if you can spot it!

Max's Extra Jupiter Fact

The Great Red Spot rotates once every six days and it spins counterclockwise.

Xing's Jupiter Math Problem

Take a look at the planets and the tilt of their axis. Which planet has the largest tilt? Which has the smallest? Can you put them in order of tilt?

Mercury	0.01°
Venus	177°
Earth	23°
Mars	25°
Jupiter	3°
Saturn	27°
Uranus	98°
Neptune	28°

Answer: Venus, Uranus, Neptune, Saturn, Mars, Earth, Jupiter, Mercury.

Stella's Jupiter Picture Gallery

Here we can see an aurora over the northern pole of Jupiter. It's made by charged particles from the Sun hitting the atmosphere.

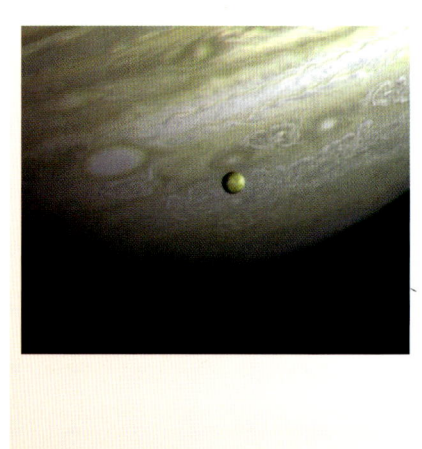

This is the moon Io orbiting in front of Jupiter.

Mo's Research Project

Find out about space missions to Jupiter. What did they discover and are there any future missions planned?

Juno space probe, orbiting Jupiter

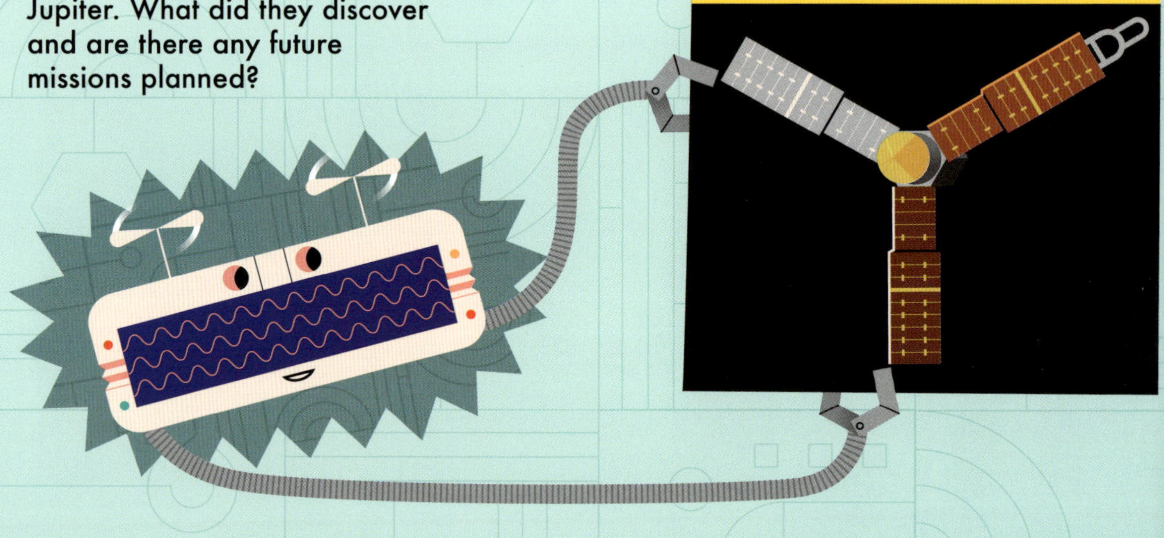

The storms on Jupiter are very clear in this picture. We can see the Great Red Spot, swirls of cloud, and white and gray storm spots.

These are the moons we visited. Clockwise from top left: Ganymede, Europa, Io, and Callisto. They're not really this close together!

Further Information

Wonderful websites
spaceplace.nasa.gov/all-about-jupiter/en/
solarsystem.nasa.gov/planets/jupiter/overview/

Awesome books
Dr. Maggie's Grand Tour of the Solar System by Dr. Maggie Aderin-Pocock (Buster Books, 2019)
So Many Questions About Space by Sally Spray (Wayland, 2022)
Wonders of the Night Sky by Professor Raman Prinja (Wayland, 2022)

Glossary

asteroid belt—the area of space where most small, rocky objects called asteroids are found
atmosphere—the layer of gas surrounding a planet
axis—the imaginary line around which an object, such as a planet, rotates
comet—a lump of ice, dust, and rock that orbits the Sun
core—the center of something, such as a planet
crater—a large, bowl-shaped hole in the surface of something, such as a moon
diameter—the measurement across the middle of a sphere or circle
gravity—the force of attraction that pulls one thing toward another
interstellar—describes something that is located or happens between stars
Jovian—relating to Jupiter
meteor—a space rock that appears as a streak of light as it falls through a planet's atmosphere
molecules—a group of atoms forming the smallest part of something
moon—a natural body that orbits a planet
orbit—the path a planet or moon takes around a star or planet
solar system—the Sun and the objects in orbit around it

Index

asteroid belt 9
asteroids 11
axis 29

comets 9, 11, 13, 14, 16
craters 20, 22, 24

dust 8, 18
dwarf planets 7

Earth 6, 7, 9, 10, 17, 22, 24, 26, 29

gases 8, 10, 11, 13

ice 20, 22, 23, 24

Jupiter 4–13, 15, 17, 18,-21, 28, 29, 30, 31

Jupiter (continued)
    atmosphere 10, 11, 12, 14, 18, 30
    core 8, 11
    day 6
    diameter 7
    formation 8-9
    gravity 11, 15, 17, 26
    Great Red Spot 10, 14, 31
    moons 18, 19, 20-27, 30, 31
    rings 18, 19
    size 7
    storms 10, 13, 31
    stripes 10
    weather 13
    year 6

lava 27

Mars 7, 8, 29
Mercury 7, 20, 29
meteors 18

orbit 8, 18
oxygen 20, 22, 24

pressure 16
primitive life 24

saltwater 20, 24
solar system 4, 7, 8, 9, 22, 24, 26
star 13
Sun 6, 7, 8, 13, 18, 24, 30

telescope 6, 26

volcanoes 26